BIG SPORTS BRANDS

NIKE

Sportswear and Brand-Building Powerhouse

by Rebecca Rowell

SportsZone

An Imprint of Abdo Publishing
abdobooks.com

abdobooks.com

Published by Abdo Publishing, a division of ABDO, PO Box 398166, Minneapolis, Minnesota 55439. Copyright © 2024 by Abdo Consulting Group, Inc. International copyrights reserved in all countries. No part of this book may be reproduced in any form without written permission from the publisher. SportsZone™ is a trademark and logo of Abdo Publishing.

Printed in the United States of America, North Mankato, Minnesota.
052023
092023

Cover Photo: Phil Cole/Allsport/Getty Images Sport/Getty Images
Interior Photos: Clive Brunskill/Getty Images Sport/Getty Images, 4–5; Jakub Porzycki/NurPhoto/Getty Images, 7; Jessica Hill/AP Images, 8–9; EU/BT/Alamy, 10; Stephen Chung/Alamy Live News/Alamy, 12; PCN Black/PCN Photography/Alamy, 13; Bettmann/Getty Images, 15, 16–17; Focus on Sport/Getty Images, 18; Edward Berthelot/Getty Images Entertainment/Getty Images, 20; John Sciulli/WireImage/Getty Images, 21; Serge Attal/The Chronicle Collection/Getty Images, 23; Steve Powell/Hulton Archive/Getty Images, 24–25; Brad Smith/ISI Photos/Getty Images Sport/Getty Images, 27; Paul Severn/Allsport/Getty Images Sport/Getty Images, 28; Kirby Lee/AP Images, 30; Rick Bowmer/AP Images, 31; Robert Alexander/Archive Photos/Getty Images, 32–33; Harry How/Getty Images Sport/Getty Images, 34; Jordan Mansfield/Getty Images for Nike/Getty Images Sport/Getty Images, 35; Jaap Arriens/NurPhoto via Getty Images, 36; Peter Charlesworth/LightRocket/Getty Images, 38; Visual China Group/Getty Images, 41

Editors: Steph Giedd and Priscilla An
Series Designer: Joshua Olson

Library of Congress Control Number: 2022949051

Publisher's Cataloging-in-Publication Data

Names: Rowell, Rebecca, author.
Title: Nike: sportswear and brand-building powerhouse / by Rebecca Rowell
Other title: sportswear and brand-building powerhouse
Description: Minneapolis, Minnesota: Abdo Publishing Company, 2024 | Series: Big sports brands | Includes online resources and index.
Identifiers: ISBN 9781098290696 (lib. bdg.) | ISBN 9781098276874 (ebook)
Subjects: LCSH: Nike (Firm)--Juvenile literature. | Sports--Equipment and supplies--Juvenile literature. | Brand name products--Juvenile literature. | Sports clothing industry--Juvenile literature.
Classification: DDC 658.827--dc23

TABLE OF CONTENTS

Chapter One

FAMOUS WORLDWIDE

Hailey sat high in the stands. She was surrounded by people who seemed just as excited as she was, including her parents and sister. She was at the 2022 US Open tennis tournament, and the stadium was packed. She could not see a single empty seat. What she could see was person after person wearing that familiar logo, the Nike Swoosh. She saw it on shoes, shirts, and hats. She looked down for a moment and saw the Swoosh on her own feet and smiled.

Wearing Nike was a no-brainer. Her favorite tennis player, the person she was about to watch play a

Serena Williams started her partnership with Nike in 2003.

match, wore Nike. Serena Williams had sported Nike attire for years. She even worked with Nike to design tennis outfits. That made Hailey admire her tennis idol even more.

Hailey started playing tennis at a young age. She loved the sport, Williams, and Nike. Hailey had Nike shoes, Nike clothes, and a Nike backpack. Hailey even had a Nike jacket designed by Williams. It was comfortable and sporty, perfect for playing tennis. It just so happened to be her favorite jacket made by her favorite player.

Most Popular

Nike started in the early 1960s under a different name and as a shoe manufacturer. It wasn't until 1972 that the first Nike-branded shoe was released. Over the years, the company grew larger. It even acquired other big-name companies. Now, several decades later, the brand offers dozens of styles of shoes and has stores in more than 170 countries. Nike also sells much more than athletic footwear. People can buy shirts and other apparel. A variety of gear, such as bags, is also available.

Mobile apps are a huge part of the brand's marketing strategy. Nike has multiple apps related to shopping, health, and fitness.

Nike is the most popular sportswear brand in the world. Fans around the globe spend tens of billions of dollars each year on Nike goods. The company outsells competitors like Adidas, Asics, Puma, and Under Armour. In 2021 Nike accounted for 43.7 percent of the sportswear market. Adidas was second with 23.7 percent. That means consumers spend almost twice as much on Nike as on Adidas. In short, Nike is far ahead of its competition.

Nike's popularity is undeniable. Even so, many fans of the brand may not know its origins. It all started in Oregon with a college coach, a wild idea, and a waffle iron.

Chapter Two

NIKE'S HUMBLE BEGINNING

The world-famous Nike Inc. began as Blue Ribbon Sports in 1964 in Beaverton, Oregon. Initially, the company sold Tiger shoes. The athletic footwear was made in Japan by Onitsuka Tiger, a company now known as Asics.

Bill Bowerman cofounded Blue Ribbon Sports with Phil Knight. The two opened their first retail store in 1966. At the time, Bowerman was the head coach of track-and-field at the University of Oregon. Knight was the company's chief executive officer, a position he held until his retirement in 2016. He had been a runner on Bowerman's team in the late 1950s.

Phil Knight retired from Nike in 2016, more than 50 years after cofounding Blue Ribbon Sports.

BASKETBALL
HALL OF FAME
ENSHRINEE

Bowerman had been focusing on running shoes for years. As a coach, he saw the issues runners faced on the track. When he began coaching at the University of Oregon in 1948, track shoes were very different. They were like leather dress shoes, the kind of footwear worn with a suit, and they had nails on the bottom. Bowerman wanted to improve this essential piece of sports equipment. Bowerman had ideas and tried to share them with different shoe companies, but no one wanted to hear his suggestions.

With no shoemakers willing to listen to him, Bowerman took a different route. He decided to make shoes himself. He tried different materials, including skin from deer, fish, and snakes. With every effort, he worked to make the shoes lighter, allowing athletes to move faster.

Knight had worn some of Bowerman's shoes while he was a student at Oregon. After Knight graduated, he went to business school at the University of Stanford in California. He wrote a paper about shoe production. Knight believed companies could earn more money if they moved labor from Germany, where most shoes at the time were produced, to Japan. After earning his degree from Stanford, Knight traveled to Japan where his partnership with Onitsuka Tiger began. Bowerman supported Knight. Together, they created Blue Ribbon Sports.

In 1965 Bowerman shared one of his own shoe designs with Onitsuka Tiger. He suggested a shoe that would provide the foot support that runners need. The company liked the idea and developed the shoe in 1967, calling it the Tiger Cortez.

Around this time, relations between Onitsuka Tiger and Blue Ribbon Sports began to deteriorate. According to Knight, Onitsuka Tiger wanted to work with distributors other than Blue Ribbon Sports. Onitsuka Tiger said Blue Ribbon Sports had created its own shoe that was too similar to the Tiger Cortez.

The two companies took their fight to court. A judge made the decision that both companies could have a version of the Cortez. The two companies parted ways in 1971. The Nike Cortez dropped in 1972 and became a bestseller.

Nike Is Born

The separation from Onitsuka Tiger marked a new era for Blue Ribbon Sports. Bowerman and Knight wanted to rebrand the company. But they needed a new name. Knight wanted to call the company Dimension Six. Jeff Johnson, Blue Ribbon Sports's first employee, coined the name Nike. Nike was the ancient Greek goddess of victory. On May 30, 1971, Blue Ribbon Sports became Nike, Inc.

The company also needed a new logo. That came from Carolyn Davidson, a design student at Portland State University. She designed the now-famous Swoosh. It became Nike's official logo and received a US patent on June 18, 1971.

Bill Bowerman's Waffle Trainer revolutionized track shoes.

That same year, Bowerman had a wild idea. One morning while making breakfast, he linked the waffles he and his wife were making to track and field. One challenge with running shoes was getting a good grip on the track. Bowerman thought runners might run faster if track shoes had a pattern on their soles. Bowerman wanted to make shoes with a waffle-bottomed pattern on the soles.

Bowerman put his wife's waffle iron to a new use. He poured melted urethane into the appliance to work on his idea for soles. Bowerman's efforts led to the Waffle Trainer. It featured the Swoosh and was used by runners at the 1972 US Olympic trials for track and field. Nike began selling the Waffle Trainer commercially in 1973.

In 1972 Nike officially signed its first professional athlete, tennis player Ilie Năstase. He would be the first of thousands of athletes to endorse the brand. The 1980s brought Nike a new era of success with the signing of an endorsement deal with National Basketball Association (NBA) star Michael Jordan in 1984. At that time, few basketball players had signature shoes.

The partnership with Jordan changed that. Nike had an idea. The company wanted to do more than name the shoe it would develop after Jordan. It would work with the athlete to design a shoe. That led to the Air Jordan 1, the first offering in what would become a line of shoes and more. As Jordan's popularity surged, so did Nike's. A few years later, in 1988, Nike introduced a new campaign: "Just Do It." Decades later, the company is still using the hugely popular slogan.

As Nike became more successful, it began acquiring other companies. In 2002 Nike bought Hurley, which makes surfing apparel, for $95 million. And in 2004 Nike spent more than $305 million to buy Converse, the footwear maker known for its Chuck Taylor All Star shoes that once dominated the NBA.

Continued Growth

Though Nike has grown significantly over the years, the company has kept its world headquarters in Beaverton. The company also has headquarters in Europe and China. A separate headquarters for Converse is in Boston, Massachusetts.

Nike continues to sign a variety of athletes. These and other partnerships have contributed to the brand's popularity and success. So has offering a variety of products to people of all ages and abilities.

Before Nike began making basketball shoes in 1972, most players wore shoes made by Converse.

Chapter Three

SHOES AND SO MUCH MORE

Nike is best known for its athletic footwear, and for good reason. Nike's partnership with basketball superstar Michael Jordan led to a sneaker culture that had not existed before. People had to have their Jordans—and countless fans still feel that way.

Jordan took the court wearing a pair of Nike Air Ship shoes on October 18, 1984. The shoes caught the attention of NBA officials. The league had rules for uniforms, and Jordan broke them. In addition to not matching the shoes of his teammates, Jordan's footwear was less than 51 percent white. The shoes

The black, red, and white colors of early Air Jordans matched those of Jordan's NBA team—the Chicago Bulls.

NBA
BULLS

Nike used the NBA ban to market the Air Jordan 1, *pictured*. Before the shoe released, the company made commercials that told viewers the NBA could not stop them from wearing the Air Jordan 1.

were designed in Chicago Bulls colors, black and red, with white only along the bottom edge. The league banned them, which brought Nike attention.

In 1985 the soon-to-be NBA Rookie of the Year premiered the Air Jordan 1 at the Slam Dunk Contest, along with a black-and-red tracksuit. Nike made news of their banned shoes public. The company advertised the Air Jordan 1 as if it had been banned by the NBA. Jordan talked about the shoes with talk show host David Letterman. The marketing for the Air Jordan 1 was extremely successful. When Nike made Air Jordans available for sale later that year, consumers were eager to buy them. In Air Jordans' first 10 months on the market, sales reached $100 million.

Air Jordans were a hit and still are. Original Air Jordan 1 shoes included the Swoosh logo. The Air Jordan 2 launched in 1986. It did not include the Swoosh, though the Nike name was on the back of the shoes. The Air Jordan 3 released in 1988. It was the first shoe to feature the Jumpman logo. Today Nike's Jordan Brand is its own line and continues to create the Air Jordan 1, updating the original design with new color schemes. Nike sells the famous shoe in its original high-top version as well as in low tops. Options are available for men, women, and children. Air Jordans are designed for athletic play and everyday wear.

Beyond the Air Jordan line, Nike sells other shoes for basketball and a variety of sports and activities. These include baseball, football, soccer, and track and field. Golfing, skateboarding, and walking shoes are available too, among others. Depending on the category,

For many customers, Nike is an essential shoe in streetwear.

options may include high tops, low tops, and a variety of soles, including some with spikes. One shoe even has a pouch on the back to store small items, such as keys.

Nike's shoe collection also has casual wear. Styles include sandals, slides, and slippers. Options are available for adults and kids alike. Nike even has footwear for babies, which includes booties and shoes.

Apparel

Even though footwear is what got Nike started, the brand's apparel has brought the company further into the spotlight. Clothing options feature hoodies and pullovers, pants and leggings, shirts, and shorts. Buyers will also find socks, swimwear, and tracksuits. If someone wanted, they could dress in Nike from head to toe—and people do. In addition, Nike makes uniforms for youth sports teams up to professional teams.

Nike wants to ensure that all athletes can perform their best, so the brand also makes performance gear. This gear is specifically designed to keep the athlete comfortable during periods of high activity. Nike clothing helps keep athletes cool and dry in all types of weather.

Clothing for women has additional categories, such as jumpsuits and rompers, dresses and skirts, leggings, and sports bras. Some items, such as leggings and pullovers, include maternity options. Nike also has hijabs, including one for swimming.

Kids' clothing includes many of the same categories as those for adults. Nike also has a variety of onesies, which they call "bodysuits."

Celebrities like Hailey Bieber wear Nike's products.

Accessories and Equipment

Nike fans can express their love of the brand beyond attire. Consumers can complete their look with belts, gloves, hats, socks, and sunglasses. Nike also has bags, backpacks, and water bottles. Swimmers will find goggles and caps. Nike also creates fitness apps for the Apple Watch, along with a collection of watchbands specifically designed for athletes. The company also sells hair accessories. Options include bows, headbands, and scrunchies.

For those who want workout gear for home, Nike can help. Examples include a training belt, resistance bands, and push-up grips. Those who practice yoga can find mats. And athletes in different sports will find a variety of gloves, such as for football, golf, and soccer. Nike also makes protective gear such as shin guards. Basketballs, footballs, and soccer balls are also available for purchase.

Kids' products include many of these accessories—in smaller sizes, of course. Baby bibs are available too. And kids

A Nike storefront has its iconic logo and slogan above the door.

can go to school in Nike style thanks to a selection of kids' backpacks and lunch bags.

Many people who buy Nike do so because of the athletes they see wearing the brand. They admire their favorite sports players and teams and emulate them. Athletes have been critical to Nike's success.

Chapter Four

THE POWER OF PARTNERSHIP

Nike has been a part of countless athletes' lives. And thousands of athletes have contributed to Nike's story and success. Initially, the brand worked with runners as Bill Bowerman focused on helping those he coached achieve their best. In 1972 Nike hired its first professional athlete to officially endorse the brand, tennis star Ilie Năstase.

As Nike grew, so did its representation in different sports. Several more tennis players joined the ranks, including legends John McEnroe and Serena Williams. McEnroe has been with Nike the longest of all Nike athletes, since 1978. And Michael Jordan

American tennis star John McEnroe was ranked No. 1 in tennis from 1981 to 1984.

3.09
ROLEX
B. BORG
J.P. McENROE

catapulted Nike's popularity with basketball players. Today, many basketball stars partner with the company, including LeBron James and Kevin Durant. The list goes on and on. Nike's family of endorsers tops 16,000. That includes athletes, teams, and leagues.

Athlete Feedback

Endorsements work in two ways. The brand supports those who endorse it, and the athletes do the same in return. This is one of the reasons that Nike has such a broad roster of endorsements. The company gets to know its athletes and supports them in different ways. Examples include providing therapeutic massages, helping with custom shoes, and even providing business mentoring. In return, the athletes can provide Nike feedback about its products. As Nike marketing executive John Slusher noted, "Listening to the voice of the athlete is so crucial to us." But Nike goes beyond supporting athletes on the courts, fields, and tracks—wherever they play. Alex Morgan is an example.

Morgan is a US professional soccer player who signed an endorsement contract with Nike in 2011. She had been a fan of Nike since childhood and even founded a Nike club with two friends at the age of seven. She described getting an endorsement contract with Nike as "a dream come true." For all the support the partnership brought her as an athlete, Morgan's favorite experience came when she stopped playing soccer in 2019 to have a baby. That year, Nike released a new product line of maternity clothing. As Nike was developing the line, the company gave Morgan items to wear. She described the experience: "Just to feel supported—not only on the field but as a mom-to-be—that felt really good."

Nike cofounder Phil Knight explained the company's approach to working with athletes in this way:

Alex Morgan helped the US women's soccer team win an Olympic gold medal as well as two World Cups.

Professional golfer Tiger Woods is one of Nike's endorsed athletes.

We take the time to understand our athletes, and we have to build long-term relationships with them. Those relationships go beyond any financial transactions. . . . We like them, and they like us. We win their hearts as well as their feet.

The listening and the support are reciprocated. Nike-endorsed athletes are required to attend a certain number of events each year as part of their contracts. However, many athletes attend more than the required number, partially due to their positive relationships with the brand.

Nike acknowledges some of its endorsed athletes by naming buildings after them. Ken Griffey Jr., Mia Hamm, and Tiger Woods are only a few. As Knight explained, "The buildings are named after the men and women who have given us more than their names and endorsements . . . they've given us our identity."

LeBron James Innovation Center

In September 2022, Nike celebrated the grand opening of the LeBron James Innovation Center. The building honors the basketball great, who has a lifetime contract with Nike. A collection of his shoes is on display, and a colorful mural depicts the basketball star. But the building is much more.

Located on the campus of Nike's world headquarters, the center is home to the Nike Sport Research Lab. The previous lab was established in 1999 in the Mia Hamm Building. The new lab is five times as big and home to dozens of employees who are part of the Advanced Innovation team. The team works with athletes and studies them in motion. The facility includes a basketball court, two running tracks, and a mini soccer field. In addition, outside is a long incline ramp.

Nike's world headquarters is in Beaverton, Oregon.

Nike researchers can study both athletes and equipment. The facility utilizes hundreds of tools and technologies to understand both. For example, four climate chambers put people and products in different environments. This helps Nike understand its clothing in different weather conditions, allowing the company to then improve its products.

Researchers also study athletes in motion using an array of cameras and force plates. The plates measure the impact bodies make when hitting the floor. One example is a runner's feet when going around a track. A runner can test different shoes, and the information from the plates, cameras, and other technologies will help the researchers and runner understand the effects of wearing those shoes.

The athletic surfaces available at the research facility are intended to be used in different ways. For example, while the

basketball court is designed for that sport, it has been used by dancers and yoga practitioners.

Regardless of the activity, the technology of the lab and the researchers using it can help athletes improve their performance. And because this testing involves Nike products, that ultimately means the research can help everyday athletes too.

Chapter Five

NEVER DONE

Nike relies on professional athletes to promote its products. But for the company to be successful, it needs people to buy those products. Everyday people are important players in Nike's story. Nike sees anyone who uses its products as an athlete, noting on its website, "If you have a body, you are an athlete."

To emphasize that idea, Nike has developed clothing that is more inclusive. For example, Nike has extended its sizing. That means the brand has more sizes than ever before, making its products available to more people.

A Nike billboard featuring football star Colin Kaepernick hangs in San Francisco. The company supported Kaepernick's outspoken stance on racial injustice in America.

Believe in something, even if
it means sacrificing everything.
Just do it.
32' X 36'
278
POST STREET INC.

The Zoom UNVRS is Nike's first FlyEase shoe.

Inclusivity also includes gender-neutral attire. The brand has shirts, hoodies, shorts, shoes, and other attire designed for any gender. The line also comes in children's sizes.

In 2021 Nike launched a new shoe with a different market in mind. For a variety of reasons, millions of people struggle to tie shoelaces or put shoes on in general. The FlyEase Go has no laces or Velcro. In fact, it does not require hands at all. Its special sole allows the wearer to step into and out of the shoe easily. And a band around the shoe helps it hold its shape and stay on the foot.

Supporting People and Causes

In recent years, the company has paid particular attention to three groups: women, youth, and runners. Nike has created more women's clothing, particularly bras and tights. The company also designed items with a new look, such as jerseys with lace trim.

Nike is focusing more on young athletes as well. That is partly because those athletes are making up an increasing percentage of the company's earnings. The brand supports youth sports by sponsoring leagues and clubs at the local level. The sponsorships lead to participants wearing Nike gear. This helps bring young consumers to the brand. Another way to do this is through professional athletes. Kids see their sports idols wearing Nike and want to wear Nike too.

Nike's "Just Do It" campaign has long encouraged people to be active in sports.

Running and runners were the cornerstone of Nike when it began. And the company continues to focus on running in terms of products. However, running items are not selling as well as the company would like. To improve the situation, Nike continues to design new shoes. Nike also seeks to win over runners by sponsoring running events.

The Nike Run Club app aids runners by featuring challenges as well as guided runs.

The company also redesigned its running app, Nike+, making it Nike Run Club. The app tracks a variety of data points, such as location, distance, elevation, and the runner's pace and heart rate. The app allows users to connect with others and to take part in running challenges.

Nike uses technology to appeal to consumers in general, not only runners. With the Nike app, users can learn about products and shop. The app also has stories about people from around the globe. The Nike app provides a personalized experience by making recommendations based on the user's searches.

Nike Training Club and SNKRS are additional Nike apps. Nike Training Club has workouts and coaching as well as wellness articles, such as nutrition information. SNKRS, as the name suggests, is about Nike sneakers. Users can get information about their favorite shoes from Nike and stay up to date on new designs, including when they will be available for purchase.

Extending beyond sports, Nike is committed to people and causes. Nike's Black Community Commitment is working to promote racial equality for Black people. The company has given millions of dollars to dozens of groups to strengthen and empower Black communities. In 2022 Nike announced that it planned to give $7.75 million throughout the fiscal year to a variety of organizations that support Black communities.

Nike supported national organizations too. All Star Code is a nonprofit that teaches computer programming to young men of color. The skills create job opportunities for participants. Danny Rojas, who heads All Star Code, said the money would help the organization reach more youth of color, as many as 100,000 people.

Controversies

In its pursuit of success, Nike has had its controversies. During the 1990s, it came to light that Nike was using exploitative factories called sweatshops to make its shoes. In one case, workers in Indonesia made as little as 14 cents an hour. Other reports stated that Nike factories used child labor.

Some people responded by holding protests, including at Nike stores. Sales dropped so much that Nike had to lay off workers. Nike responded by acknowledging the problem and then improving it by paying workers more and making factories better. This helped improve consumers' perceptions of the brand.

However, a 2020 *Washington Post* opinion article stated that Nike factory employees in China were forced to work

Workers produce Nike shoes in Ho Chi Minh City in Vietnam.

in prisonlike conditions. The authors wrote that these labor practices were likely used by other major brands too. They stated China's government had placed hundreds of thousands of people in detention camps since 2017. The government then sent tens of thousands of them to different areas of China to do factory work, including at a Nike factory.

Another issue involved athletes. In 2019 Nike ended its long-distance running program after its coach, Alberto Salazar, was accused of giving athletes performance-enhancing drugs. The Nike Oregon Project began in 2001 and trained top-level runners. The US Anti-Doping Agency banned Salazar from the sport for four years.

Nike Athlete Think Tank

In early 2022, Nike created the Nike Athlete Think Tank. It consists of 13 female athletes from around the world representing several sports. They will help Nike address the disparity and barriers that exist for women in sports. Nike pledged $1.3 million to help create opportunities for girls and women. Nike donated the money to 20 charities and organizations that were chosen by the athletes.

In addition to the doping scandal, runner Mary Cain said Salazar was emotionally abusive when she trained with him. In response, Nike announced that it would investigate the situation. The company said it would use the information from the investigation to improve how Nike works with and helps female athletes. Nike promotes sports participation for girls and women. The company supports more than 135 community groups that support women and girls around the globe.

In 2019 track star Allyson Felix shared a painful experience she had with Nike. Felix's contract with Nike expired in December 2017. When negotiating a new contract, Felix shared that she planned to start a family in 2018. Nike offered Felix a lot less money during negotiations. The company would not promise to support her if she was not a top performer in the months following childbirth. Felix left Nike and joined Athleta. After Felix shared her story, Nike responded by changing its maternity policy to help the company's athletes.

Thinking Ahead

Nike's work is also focused on doing what's best for the planet. The company is working on circular design, which tries to eliminate waste. It also aims to have as small a carbon footprint as possible. Nike even has a Circular Design Guide it makes available to anyone.

Nike's ISPA Link shoe is the result of Nike's environmentally minded design efforts. Unlike other shoe designs, the ISPA Link does not use glue. This reduces the time and energy it takes to construct the shoe. It also makes the product easier to take apart and recycle. Because of glue, shoes typically need to be

Basketball star LeBron James signed a lifetime contract with Nike in 2015.

shredded before they can be recycled. This process takes a lot of energy. The Link Axis shoe is made from recycled materials. When the shoes are worn out, consumers can take them to a Nike store that has a recycling and donation service to be recycled.

For decades, "Just Do It" has served as Nike's tagline. In 2022 Nike celebrated its 50th anniversary. In honor of its golden anniversary, the brand developed a new slogan: "Never Done." Given the strength of the brand with consumers and athletes, Nike looks ahead to more growth over the next 50 years.

TIMELINE

1964

Blue Ribbon Sports begins as a shoe distributor for Tiger shoes, footwear made by Japanese shoemaker Onitsuka Tiger.

1971

Blue Ribbon Sports becomes Nike Inc. on May 30.

1971

The Swoosh officially becomes Nike's logo. It gets a US patent on June 18.

1972

Professional tennis player Ilie Năstase becomes the first professional athlete to sign with Nike.

1984

Nike signs basketball superstar Michael Jordan to an endorsement deal.

1988

Nike introduces a new campaign: "Just Do It."

2019

Nike ends its Oregon Project, the company's long-distance training program, when its head coach is banned from the sport for doping.

2022

Nike celebrates its 50th anniversary.

IMPORTANT PEOPLE

Bill Bowerman

Coach Bill Bowerman cofounded Nike. He created the Waffle Trainer running shoe using a waffle iron from his home. While coaching for the University of Oregon, he led his team to four college championships and created the All-Comers Meet for runners of all ages.

Carolyn Davidson

Carolyn Davidson is credited with creating the Nike Swoosh. She was a design student at Portland State University.

LeBron James

Basketball star LeBron James has a lifetime contract with Nike. The company's Beaverton research facility, LeBron James Innovation Center, is named after him.

Jeff Johnson

Jeff Johnson was Blue Ribbon Sports's first employee and came up with the company's name.

Michael Jordan

Basketball legend Michael Jordan is Nike's highest-paid athlete. He worked with Nike to create his line of Air Jordan products. His relationship with the company has contributed to Nike's success.

Phil Knight

Phil Knight cofounded Nike with Bill Bowerman. He ran the business side of Nike and created the company's beginning partnership with Onitsuka Tiger. Knight was the chief executive officer of Nike until he retired in 2016.

John McEnroe

Tennis legend John McEnroe has been with Nike the longest, since 1978.

Serena Williams

Tennis superstar Serena Williams is a Nike athlete and has partnered with the company to design some of her tennis outfits.

GLOSSARY

carbon footprint
The amount of greenhouse gases created when doing something; these gases harm the planet.

distributor
A person or company that buys a product from the manufacturer and sells it to consumers.

doping
To use a banned drug to perform better at a sport.

emulate
To imitate, or copy, someone.

endorse
To promote a company in exchange for their products or money.

hijab
A hair covering worn by Muslim girls and women.

maternity
Related to pregnancy.

patent
A document from the US government giving someone the exclusive right to make and sell something.

sweatshop
A factory in which employees work many hours in poor conditions for little pay.

tagline
Words that become associated with a brand or product; a slogan.

urethane
A flexible substance used in many products, including shoes and clothing.

BOOKS

Kinley, J. R. *Adidas: Athletic Apparel Trailblazer*. Minneapolis, MN: Abdo Publishing, 2024.

Knight, Phil. *Shoe Dog: Young Readers Edition*. New York: Simon & Schuster, 2017.

Mason, Tyler. *Michael Jordan and the Chicago Bulls*. Minneapolis, MN: Abdo Publishing, 2019.

ONLINE RESOURCES

To learn more about Nike, please visit **abdobooklinks.com** or scan this QR code. These links are routinely monitored and updated to provide the most current information available.

INDEX

ABOUT THE AUTHOR

Rebecca Rowell has put her degree in publishing and writing to work as an editor and as an author, working on dozens of books. Recent topics as an author include the world's wildfires and dealing with family challenges. She lives in Minneapolis, Minnesota.